$.34

Cruelty, sadness
in ch. books

RUDYARD KIPLING

RUDYARD KIPLING
(Courtesy of Radio Times Hulton Picture Library)

Rudyard Kipling

A WALCK MONOGRAPH

by

Rosemary Sutcliff

HENRY Z. WALCK, INCORPORATED
NEW YORK

© The Bodley Head Ltd 1960
First American edition 1961
Printed in Great Britain

CONTENTS

A Note About the Author

Rosemary Sutcliff's father was a naval officer and she and her mother followed him round the world until he retired when she was ten. Of her early life she writes, 'My schooling began late, owing to a childhood illness, and ended when I was only fourteen, owing to my entire lack of interest in being educated. But I showed signs of being able to paint, and so from school I went to art school, trained hard, and eventually became a professional miniature painter. I did not start to write until the end of the War, but now I have switched completely from one medium to the other, and it is several years since I last touched paint.'

Rosemary Sutcliff has written ten children's books, and one, *The Lantern Bearers*, was awarded the 1959 Carnegie Medal. Of this present book she says, 'My reason for writing this monograph will be obvious to anyone who reads it: I have loved Kipling for as long as I can remember.'

1. Early Days

In the High and Far Off days when the Indian Mutiny was only seven years past and the Indian Empire only seven years old, a son was born to John Lockwood Kipling, Principal of the new School of Art in Bombay. He was a first child, and his parents called him Rudyard after the lake beside which they had done most of their courting.

Rudyard Kipling's first few years were lived in a bungalow in the compound of the School of Art, uncomfortably near to the Towers of Silence on which the Parsees exposed their dead to the vultures —so uncomfortably near that unconsidered bits of dead Parsee were constantly falling into the garden. The ayah who looked after his little sister was a Goanese Roman Catholic, and used often to take him to the chapel of her faith. Meeta, the bearer, was a Hindu, and took him just as often to the temple of Shiva; and he went to either place of worship with equal willingness. Indeed, all his life he never followed completely the teachings of any one faith, and perhaps his free thinking had its beginnings in this richly varied religious upbringing of his earliest years.

For Service families, or families whose business

9

keeps them in hot countries, there are nearly always agonising partings to be faced as the children grow older, and when Rudyard was five and his little sister not yet three, there was a trip to England from which the parents returned alone, leaving the children as paying guests in the house of a retired naval officer at Southsea. Why they were left to the care of strangers is a mystery. One of Mrs Kipling's sisters was married to a rich ironmaster, Alfred Baldwin, another—the adored Aunt Georgie —to Burne-Jones, and the third to Sir Edward Poynter, afterwards President of the Royal Academy. They all had children and they were devoted sisters, and the obvious thing would have seemed to be for one of them to take Rudyard and Trix.

The six years that he spent in Southsea were the most wretched of Kipling's whole life, and he emerged from them having used up his whole supply of hate on the mistress of the house (whom he writes of in his autobiography as 'The Woman'), so that he was never able to feel a really full-blooded hate for anyone else. Trix, the little sister, did well enough in the 'House of Desolation'; it was only Rudyard who, for some unknown reason, came in for the full force of The Woman's zeal for the rooting out of sin, and him she terrified with Hell

Fire and sought to reform with punishments and persecutions through all those six years.

But in each year there was one shining month which he and Trix spent with Aunt Georgie, a month during which they lived, so far as the nursery of those days could live, in the society of the adult world, of men like Burne-Jones and William Morris: William Morris, who, finding the aunt and uncle out one day when he called, came up to the school-room, and, seated creakingly majestic on the ancient rocking-horse, regaled its inhabitants with the story-outline of the Saga of Burnt Njal.

The one other shining thing in those dark years was that at some point in them the child Rudyard discovered what reading was about. When he could read, a friend of The Woman's gave him a little purple book called *The Hope of the Katzikopfs*. It was of severely moral tone, but it contained verses that began 'Farewell Rewards and Fairies', from which seed came flower and fruit at a later date.

The end of the Southsea period came when the small boy's eyes went wrong. He was found to be half blind and on the edge of some kind of break-down; his mother returned from India un-expectedly, and when she came to his bedside and bent to kiss him goodnight, he flung up his arm to ward off the blow he had grown to expect. That was the end of The Woman, and the beginning of five years at the United Service College, at Westward Ho! on the North Devon coast.

Cormell Price, the headmaster, was a personal friend of the Kiplings, which made the choice an obvious one, and this time all went well. The College had been started only a few years before by a handful of Service officers wanting a cheap but sound education for their sons, but though it was founded by Service officers and most of its boys went into one or other of the Services in their turn, anything less like a military academy could scarcely be imagined. There were no parades, no uniforms, no bands or flags—indeed for the school's opinion of such things one has only to read the chapter in *Stalky & Co.* which deals with the Jelly-bellied Flag-flapper. The school buildings had been converted from a terrace of twelve bleak lodging houses; the food 'would have provoked a mutiny in Dartmoor today'; it was a hard school, but most of its boys remembered it afterwards with love. Certainly Kipling did.

Into the midst of the United Service College he burst at the age of not quite twelve, a small boy with an enormous smile, a pair of bright blue eyes behind very thick spectacles which immediately gained him the name of Gig-lamps, and already the first faint foreshadowing of a moustache. On his very first day he made common cause with a bony-faced Irish boy, George Beresford by name, and before his first year was out, the two were joined by 'Stalky' Dunsterville. Thereafter, the three went up the school together, frequently at war amongst themselves, but presenting a united and extremely formidable front to the rest of the world.

They were to be in later years the Beetle, Mac-Turk and Stalky of *Stalky & Co.*, a book which abounds in portraits and semi-portraits.

At the end of the 1882 summer term the schoolboy triumvirate broke up, and the future took them
their separate ways; Dunsterville to be a soldier,
Beresford a civil engineer, Kipling at the age of
sixteen and three-quarters, to sail for India and a
job as assistant editor of the *Civil and Military
Gazette*, published in Lahore.

His father and mother had lately moved to Lahore
from Bombay, and John Lockwood Kipling was
now Principal of the School of Art and Curator of
the Museum, which stood, just as described in
Kim, beside the Mall running from the European
quarter to the old native city. So young Kipling
lived with his parents, but had his own room, his
own servant, his own horse and dog-cart, and (glory
of glories!) his own office-box to take to work every
morning. And when a year or so later Trix came
out to join them, the whole family were united
again.

The job of assistant editor meant in fact that
young Kipling was 'fifty per cent of the editorial
staff' and worked hours accordingly, ten to fifteen
of them a day. But somehow, especially when his
family had gone up to the hills for the hot weather,
where he could only follow them for a month out

of the three or four that they would be away, he found time to rediscover India. Chiefly at night, the dark hot fever-smelling nights when nobody could sleep and much of the life of Lahore went on in the streets or on the roof tops, he would explore the ancient Muslim city crouched under the grim square fortress reeking of many ghosts, from which Ranjit Singh, the Lion of the Punjab, had ruled his short-lived Sikh kingdom. And these night-time prowlings, as well as the odder side of his newspaper work, brought him many unusual friends. One, a certain Pathan horse dealer named Mahbub Ali, later to become familiar to readers of *Kim*, a man of 'indescribable filth but magnificent mien and features', brought him news of Central Asia beyond the Khyber Pass. He also got to know both officers and men of the British Infantry companies which now garrisoned the old Sikh fort; and at the Lahore Club he sat among representatives of the Army, Education, Canals, Forestry, Engineering, Irrigation, Railways, Medicine and Law, all talking in great detail their own particular brand of 'shop'. And all these things and people played a part in making him the kind of writer that he afterwards became.

Three years after he came out from England, he began writing short stories for the *Civil and Military*

Gazette, under the collective title of *Plain Tales from the Hills*, which were used as and when extra material was needed. And the thing had begun. In 1887 he was transferred to the staff of the *Pioneer* at Allahabad, where, stimulated by the change, he promptly wrote the horrifyingly precocious *Story of the Gadsbys*. His new job entailed a good deal of travelling about Northern India in search of copy, including a visit to the Rajput States of the Indian Desert, which filled his notebooks with local colour. And on this trip a few hours spent in the abandoned city of Amber furnished him with the 'Cold Lairs' of the *Jungle Books*.

But the Indian phase of Kipling's life was closing and another opening to him, as his writing became better known. By the end of 1889 he was in London again; and in London, like Lord Byron before him, he woke up one morning to find himself famous. His *Ballad of East and West*, that most often quoted and misquoted of all his works, was published in November, and from then on, everything he wrote was eagerly sought after. He began to meet all the great literary figures of the day; he began to make so much money that soon he had a whole thousand pounds in the bank, and got his beloved family home on a short visit to share his astonished delight.

At that time also he met Walcott Balestier, a young American agent for a New York firm of publishers, and struck up a devoted friendship with him, which resulted, among other things, in their combining to write *The Naulahka*.

This friendship led also to a meeting with Balestier's sister Carrie; and long before *The Naulahka* was published, the two of them had reached 'an understanding'. But there was still no formal engagement when Kipling set off on a voyage that was intended to take him round the world and return him for a while to his own folk in Lahore. After some time in South Africa, Australia and New Zealand, he reached Lahore just before Christmas 1891, but hardly had he done so when he received word from Carrie that Walcott was dead. He left at once, and was back in England a fortnight later. He never saw India again.

Within a week, he and Carrie were married by special licence; Carrie, according to eye witness reports, in 'a brown woollen dress with buttons all down the front'. Most of Kipling's friends, and certainly his mother, were more than doubtful of how this marriage to a clever, dominating and rather hard woman three years older than himself was going to work out, but it worked out, on the whole, very happily. After a honeymoon trip dramatically cut short by an unforeseen failure of funds, they settled down in a farm cottage near the little town of Brattleborough in Vermont, which was Carrie's home ground. And there, in late autumn of 1892, with snow piled to the windowsills and Carrie in process of having a baby, Kipling wrote a boy-and-wolf story called *Mowgli's Brothers*.

III. Best Beloved

The original impulse for *Mowgli's Brothers* was derived, so say both Kipling and Rider Haggard, from a scene in Haggard's *Nada the Lily*, in which Umslopogaas, the Zulu hero, runs with a wolf pack; but the whole process of thought leading on from that impulse to become the *Jungle Books* with their hero swinging between two worlds, and their strange ethical concept, the Law of the Jungle, is all Kipling's own. In this one, alone of all his books, the topography and local colour are second-hand, for the background of the Mowgli stories is along the banks of the Waingunga River in the Seonee district, a part of Central India which he had never visited. He worked, in that little snowbound New England cottage, from descriptions and photographs sent to him four years earlier by some friends; just as he took his wild animals and Indian lore from his father's knowledge of all things Indian and from Sterndale's *Mammalia of India*. The wonderful thing is that one would never guess it.

The Jungle Book was finished at the tail end of the year, about the time that little Josephine, her father's Best Beloved, came into the world; *The Second Jungle Book* two and a half years later. It seems worth noticing that out of Kipling's long writing life of more than fifty years, all his stories for children, and the stories that, though not specifically written for children are read and loved by them, were written in the seventeen or eighteen years between the time when his first child was on the way and the time when his last child was too old to have stories written for it any more.

In 1894 when *The Second Jungle Book* was still being written, there was a visit to England, and to Kipling's parents, who had by now retired and were living in the little Wiltshire village of Tisbury. In the Tisbury cottage, under his father's eye (John Lockwood was always his son's severest as well as favourite critic) the most delicate of all the stories of the *Jungle Books*, not a Mowgli story at all, but the exquisite *Miracle of Purun Bhagat* was written.

When the family returned to Vermont, it was to a big newly-built timber house of their own, 'The Naulahka', and there, in 1896, Elsie was born. By then the idea for *Kim* was stirring in Kipling's mind, but refused to come down out of the void and take shape, and shortly after visits from the local doctor to Carrie and the new baby turned his creative energies for the time being into another channel. Dr Conland had been to sea in his youth, and would sit, after his official visits, yarning about his young days and the fishermen of the Grand

Banks; from which yarns grew a book called *Captains Courageous*. That book took them, as Kipling writes in his autobiography,

'To the shore front, and the old T wharf of Boston Harbour, and to queer meals in sailors' eating houses, where he renewed his youth among ex-shipmates and their kin. We assisted hospitable tug-masters to help three- and four-stick schooners of Pochahontas coal all round the harbour; we boarded every craft that looked as if she might be useful, and we delighted ourselves to the limit of delight.'

But in spite of the children and the books growing up in it, 'The Naulahka' remained only a house and never became a home; there was trouble with Carrie's younger brother who lived close by, and small-town life, where all things political were linked with anti-British feeling, was not the life for Kipling, not the standpoint from which he could write. So once again an old phase ended and a new one began.

They arrived in England at summer's end of 1896, and took a house at Torquay. There, after Sir George Robertson, the hero of the siege of Chitral, had been to them on a visit, and his thoughts were full of Frontier fighting, Kipling wrote *Slaves of the Lamp* which in the end made the final episode of *Stalky & Co.* and having begun at the end, added the earlier chapters from time over the next three years. But neither he nor Carrie was ever happy at 'Rock House', and after eight months they fled from Torquay to Rottingdean, a little half-lost downland village in those days, where the Burne-Jones Aunt and Uncle and the Baldwin Cousin (afterwards Prime Minister) had their holiday houses. The Kiplings' son, John, was born in the Burne-Jones' house on a summer night in 1899, and soon after they rented 'The Elms' across the village green, which was to be their home for five years.

Meanwhile *Kim* had begun to stir again, more insistently this time, and that autumn Kipling took his idea for a story about the son of an Irish soldier plunged into the drifting life of wayfaring India up to Tisbury to be 'smoked over' with his father; and a little later, back at 'The Elms', he began telling the *Just So Stories* to Josephine, for whom all the earlier ones were written. But his time for telling stories to Josephine, his Best Beloved, was to be tragically short. Early 1900 brought an unexpected business trip to the U.S.A. on which Carrie insisted on taking the three children. All three caught whooping cough on arrival in New York, and Kipling himself went down with pneumonia, leaving Carrie to cope with all of them in a New York hotel. Josephine followed her father into pneumonia, and had not his strength to fight it. On March 6th, just as he came out of danger, the child died; and for her parents—certainly for her father—life was never quite the same again.

IV. The Fairy Ring

A few weeks after Josephine's death, the Kiplings returned to 'The Elms', and that autumn *Stalky & Co.* was published amid a storm of divided opinion. Kipling was now at the height of his fame, and trippers from Brighton had begun to discover the house where he lived; a house, moreover, where every corner, every shadowy hiding-place under the garden bushes, was charged with the memory of a little fair-haired girl. Rottingdean had lost its happiness and its charm.

The Boer War came, and swept Kipling and his wife off to South Africa, where there was plenty waiting for him to do. But that, as he might have said himself, is another story. Back at Rottingdean once more for a few months in the summer of 1901, he finished *Kim*, having carried it, in one way or another, for seven years.

South Africa had given them many new friends, including Cecil Rhodes, and from 1901 to 1908, the family's every winter was spent at their own cottage 'The Woolsack', built for them close to Rhodes's own house, 'Groote Schuur'. At 'The Woolsack' Kipling took up again the long laid aside *Just So Stories*, to tell to the other children, now that the child they had been made for was gone. And there he completed the book with *The Cat that Walked by Himself* and *The Butterfly that Stamped*.

But meanwhile, during the English half of the year, the Kiplings were carrying out a systematic all-over-Sussex search for the House of the Perfect Eaves. A search which ended at last when they came, driving a 'Victoria hooded, carriage sprung, carriage braked, single cylinder, belt driven, fixed ignition' Lanchester down an enlarged rabbit hole of a lane, and found at the bottom of it, 'Bateman's'.

Kipling describes 'Bateman's' as grey; he should know the colour of the house, for it was his home for more than thirty years, but to my mind it is warmer than grey, almost tawny. A warm and welcoming house of many gables and more chimneys, with the date 1634 over the door, and a dovecot like a small fortress at the back; and over all and through all, an atmosphere, gentle and quiet, made up of many layers of time. Not only the house, but the whole valley, was gloriously rich in the past of Sussex; at the bottom of a newly sunk well they turned up the bronze cheek-piece of a Roman bridle. Dredging out a choked pond produced two Elizabethan 'Sealed Quarts' and a Neolithic axehead. On the fringe of 'Bateman's' land, in a little lost valley, 'stood the long overgrown slag heap of a most ancient forge, supposed to have been worked by the Phoenicians and Romans, and since then, uninterruptedly till the middle of the eighteenth century. The bracken and rush-patches still hid stray pigs of iron, and if one scratched a few inches through the rabbit-shaven turf, one came on the narrow mule-track of peacock-hued furnace-slag laid down in Elizabeth's day. The ghost of a road climbed up out of this dead arena, and crossed our fields, where it was known as "The Gunway" and popularly connected with Armada times. Every foot of that little corner was alive with ghosts and shadows.'

Every foot of it, too, must have been alive for Kipling with the raw material of creative magic. For some time the idea of a book of stories from English history had been stirring in his mind, and he had taken it, as usual, to 'smoke over' with his father. And then in their third October at 'Bateman's,' Elsie and John decided to perform a 'Play of Puck and Titania', for which their father asked a friend in London to get them a paper donkey's head for Bottom. For stage they had a fairy ring beside the brook, at the foot of the grassy spur which they had christened 'Pook's Hill'. (There are several Pook's Hills in Sussex, but that, until the Kiplings came, does not seem to have been one of them.) And so both the setting and the mechanics of magic for *Puck of Pook's Hill* presented itself. By the following January Kipling was hard at work, and *Puck*, together with *Rewards and Fairies*, took up a large part of his attention for the next five years. The first tale in his mind, based on a suggestion from a cousin, was about a Roman centurion called Parnesius, but the Norman and Saxon stories of Sir Richard Dalyngridge materialised first, and Parnesius came later, walking out of the little wood above the Phoenician forge. The rest followed in due order. *Puck of Pook's Hill* was published in 1906, and then came a pause while the writer experimented. He tried and rejected stories about Dr Johnson, Daniel Defoe and King Arthur; but at last the eleven stories and their attendant poems which go to make up *Rewards and Fairies* were published in 1910.

The following year, when C. R. L. Fletcher's *History of England* was published, it contained songs of Kipling's that are of the same stream as those of *Puck* and *Rewards*.

Those were the last words that Kipling ever wrote for children.

And so, from the point of view of this sketch, the

story ends. But to round off neatly and in seemly fashion, in the manner of the nineteenth-century novels: John was killed at Loos in his eighteenth year; Elsie married in 1924, and the final end of the story came when Rudyard Kipling died at the age of seventy, only a day or so before his close friend King George V, and was buried in the Poet's Corner in Westminster Abbey, on January 22nd, 1936.

v. A Choice of Books

I have begun this sketch of Kipling as a writer for children with an outline of his life, because in his case, even more than most of the brotherhood, the life and the writings are bound together. Every book, every short story, has its origin in his background or the events and circumstances of his life. They came of his Indian experiences, they grew from yarnings over a pipe with a Vermont country doctor, they were written because he went to a particular school, and because he had much-loved children to tell them to.

I have left out a very great deal because it had not to do with the children's writer; journeyings to the uttermost ends of the earth, world events through which he moved and on which so many of his greatest poems were comments, the many honours that he refused and the few that he accepted. I have named scarcely any of his books, other than those written for children. I have not even mentioned *Recessional*. But all these are to be found elsewhere. A good and detailed biography is *Rudyard Kipling, his Life and Work* by Professor Charles Carrington, published by Macmillan in 1955. A magnificent study of his writing is *The Art of Rudyard Kipling* by Dr J. M. S. Tompkins, published by Methuen in 1959. Both these might well be read by those who feel like it, in conjunction with Kipling's own posthumously published autobiography, *Something of Myself*.

So far the task has been simple enough; the straightforward chronicling of facts. But the next stage is not so easy. My first difficulty has been to decide just what, out of all Kipling's works, to include among his books for children. The first half-dozen, of course, are obvious: *Stalky* and the *Just So Stories*, both *Puck* books and both *Jungle Books*. After that, *Kim* and *Captains Courageous*. These two must certainly be included, although they were not specifically written for children. But having opened the ranks to them, where to draw the line? There are magnificent stories within the capacity of an intelligent twelve- or thirteen-year-old in most of the volumes of short stories, but they are such a wondrously mixed bag that I do not think I would encourage a child to wander among them unsupervised, though I would certainly not prevent him from doing so if he really wanted to. Myself, I fell upon *Many Inventions* in my twelfth year, and revelled in it. It contains one tale, *In the Rukh*, which is simply another Mowgli story, though it was never included in the *Jungle Books*; but it contains also a hideous tragedy called *Love o'*

Women, which I read and re-read with the fascinated horror of half understanding, and which filled me with a terror of venereal disease (which I never had the sense to confide to anybody) through all my growing-up years.

So—Kipling's volumes of short stories are for the odd child here and there, but I shall not include them now; nor his one other full-length novel, *The Light that Failed*. A girl of sixteen or so may weep buckets over it, but that counts as grown-up reading. And nor shall I include '*Thy Servant, a Dog*' because I feel very strongly that it is unworthy of its writer. It is full of false sentiment, and the appalling whimsy of Boots' basic English might well put a child off the rest of Kipling for ever.

My choice then is the first and second *Jungle Books*, *Captains Courageous*, *Stalky & Co.*, *Kim*, the *Just So Stories*, *Puck of Pook's Hill* and *Rewards and Fairies*.

VI. Two Worlds

The *Jungle Books* step first upon the scene, not because they were the first to be written (I am not going to attempt to be chronological, I am simply going to arrange the books in the order in which they seem to fit most happily together), but because they were my own first introduction to Kipling. I was not more than five or six at the time, but I possessed a mother who read aloud most beautifully, and found great joy in doing it, and so from the first, I was able to enjoy books far in advance of those I could have coped with myself. From our earliest acquaintance I loved the Mowgli stories with a rather special love, not necessarily stronger, but different in kind from the love I had for any other book. I loved them for their strangeness, their 'otherness' which was somehow kept from ever getting out of bounds or becoming frightening by the familiar pattern of Mowgli's own relationships, for instance with the cosy close-drawn family life of Father and Mother Wolf and the four cubs. My feeling for the stories has of course changed with the years, without weakening; and in a way the stories themselves seem to have changed, too, for like nearly all the really great children's books, they are written on many levels,

and for me they have become a following-out of
divided life and divided loyalties, the unbearable
choice that has to be made and has to be borne.
Now also, having come to be a writer myself, I can
stand back a little and appreciate, amongst sundry
other matters, the superb craftsmanship that has
gone into creating the Jungle Folk, each one a
perfectly rounded individual (save of course for
the Monkey People, whose whole essence is that
they are not individuals at all, but merely a gibber-
ing mob) and each one perfectly within the bounds
of his own animal nature. These are not human
beings in animal skins, as even *Black Beauty*,
another love of my childhood, tends to be; nothing
so undignified. They are animals lordly in their own
right, with the innate dignity of the wild animal
who has never been taught to ride a bicycle in a
circus.

I realised, of course, precisely nothing of all that
when I was five, but I accepted the Jungle Dwellers
as dear and deeply satisfying friends, and they were
so real to me, especially Bagheera with the voice as
soft as wild honey dripping from a tree, that rem-
embering those early readings with my mother, I
can still recapture the physical sensation of the
living, sensuous, velvet-over-fire-and-steel-springs
warmth of his skin, as though I had in actual fact

33

once been on stroking terms with a black panther. I was aware also of Kipling's extraordinary power of getting under the skin of man or beast, time or place or situation, which has seemed to me ever since to be one of his greatest gifts; and I remember trying to explain to my mother what I felt about this: 'Well you see, other people write about things from the outside in, but Kipling writes about them from the inside out.' And therein lies a world of difference.

As a child I loved *The Jungle Book* best, because I knew that all would go well with the people I loved in it; I knew that even when Mowgli was turned out of the pack, he would come back to spread Shere Khan's hide on the Council Rock. But as soon as *The Second Jungle Book* was begun (my mother and I always read straight through from one to the other) I began to smell desolation in store, and even across that most wonderful story of *The King's Ankus* lay the shadow of *Red Dog* and *The Spring Running*. I could scarcely bear to listen to either of those two stories; the first battered me and tore at my heart strings with the tremendous sorrows of tragic saga, the second made my whole world ache with griefs and longings that I could not yet understand. But I am inclined to think that it does a child no harm to have its heart wrung occasionally. It broadens the mind and deepens the compassion.

At any mention of the *Jungle Books*, it is always the Mowgli stories that spring to mind; but there are of course many other stories beside. In my young days I particularly loved those of *Rikki-Tikki-Tavy* and *The White Seal* (why did the story of Kotik always seem so sad? When one comes to think of it, it had a perfectly good happy ending) which now I would exchange, both of them together, for that most lovely and strong and fragile story, *The Miracle of Purun Baghat*, which in those days was beyond my reach, as I think it would be beyond the reach of most children. But what is beyond his reach, the child will come back and reach up for again, when once his imagination has been captured; and there is in the *Jungle Books* plenty to catch at the imagination.

*　　*　　*　　*

'The lama, very straight and erect, the deep folds of his yellow clothing slashed with black in the light of the *parao* fires precisely as a knotted tree trunk is slashed with the shadows of the long sun, addressed a tinsel and lacquered *ruth* (oxcart) which burned like a many coloured jewel in the same uncertain light. The patterns on the gold-worked curtain ran up and down, melting and reforming as the folds shook and quivered in the night wind; and when the talk grew more earnest the jewelled forefinger snapped out little sparks of light between the embroideries. Behind the cart was a wall of uncertain darkness speckled with little flames and alive with half-caught forms and faces and shadows.'

I have given the quotation at length, because it expresses so perfectly two of the aspects of *Kim*. Firstly the preoccupation with light. Kipling could never visualise any incident without its attendant light and weather, season of the year and time of day; and in *Kim*, I think more than any other of his books, one is constantly aware of changing light; the wash of light across the tawny grass of a hillside, the chill grey light of dawn over waking camp or railway siding, the smoky flare of torches.

Secondly, the sense of crowding riches—riches so vast that they overflowed in all directions and much could not be used at all, though one senses them behind the rest, a shifting background 'speckled with little flames and alive with half-caught forms and faces and shadows'. Kipling himself, describing the process of smoking over the book with his father, writes:

'Under our united tobacco it grew like the Djinn released from the brass bottle, and the more we explored its possibilities the more opulence of detail did we discover. I do not know what proportion of an iceberg is below the waterline, but *Kim*, as it finally appeared, was about one tenth of what the first lavish specification called for.'

And that is exactly the impression that the reader gets.

Superficially *Kim* is a spy story, and such plot as it has concerns a boy's education to be a Secret Service agent. But the plot is little more than a thread on which to string jewels as fascinating and curious as any in the shop of Lurgan Sahib, 'The Healer of Sick Pearls'. This is why the magnificent and vastly expensive film made from the book some years ago was merely the husk, though a colourful and entertaining husk, with all the peculiar essence of *Kim* drained out of it. The film was a spy story, but *Kim* is so infinitely more. It is a drifting among the drifting vagabond life of India, too far down to be coloured by any question of state or politics, so evocative that reading it one catches the very scent of dust and withered marigolds and the smoke of little dung fires where the village worthies gather under the peepul tree in the dusk. It has a great deal of beauty, sheer spiritual beauty, and the deep-seeing time-free mysticism of the East, but it is never for an instant guilty of being solemn. No book which had the shameless Kim for its hero could be solemn.

It has a certain kinship with the *Jungle Books*. Kim is situated just as Mowgli is, a boy belonging to one world, thrown into and accepted by another, and faced in the end by the same choice to be made. Mowgli has to choose between the Jungle and the Village, Kim between going back to the world of action for which he has been trained, and remaining in the completely Eastern world to which he has wandered with his beloved lama; and though we are not specifically told so, we know that he too will go back to the Village, leaving the Jungle behind him, and that he too will break his heart in doing it. Like Mowgli, too, Kim has his sponsors in his adoptive world, four of them; foremost the lama himself, surely the most perfectly good character that Kipling ever created; the lean, ferocious Pathan horse dealer, Mahbub Ali; the smooth soft-bellied Bengali Babu with the heart of a lion, and the masterful old dowager from Saharumpore, whose constant chatter so much bothered the lama.

Kim is I think chiefly for the older child (it was not, when all's said and done, written for children at all), and not every child, even of those who like Kipling, will appreciate it. But those who do will probably get drunk on it, as I did. It is a heady brew, with its constantly changing scenes, its smells and colour and crowding drift of events and people and half-glimpsed glories. But it is the kind of drunkenness which any child would be the richer for afterward.

Stalky & Co. failed entirely with me at our first acquaintance, maybe because I was a little too young for it, though I *was* ten, but chiefly I think because my mother read it to me, and of all Kipling's stories it is the only one that does not seem to me to read aloud well. Maybe it is too full of primitive noises, the war chants of,

> 'Ti-yi! Tungalee!
> I eat um pea! I pick um pea!'

with its answering defiance, 'Ingle-go-jang, my joy, my joy!' being notable examples.

A year or so later I read it again, to myself this time, fell instantly under its spell, and must have re-read it with the delight of returning to old friends, and with much unholy laughter, at least a dozen times since them. It was something quite new in school stories, as the *Jungle Books* were something quite new in animal stories; the first of a new kind of book altogether (*Huckleberry Finn* is another of the brotherhood) which combine minute correctness of detail in depicting a way of life, together with a heightening of all its exploits. No ordinary schoolboy could bring off the diabolical exploits which Stalky, Turkey and Beetle carry through to a triumphant conclusion, but they are the kind that every schoolboy dreams of carrying through, like the perfect retort that one thinks of when it is just too late to use it. The book was greeted by a storm of contradictory opinion when it first appeared, for its casual brutalities and its somewhat harsh realism shocked a generation with more evangelical ideas of what a school book should be, and who feared that it would have a demoralising effect on the young. *Tom Brown's Schooldays* has more of really beastly cruelty in it by far than *Stalky* has, but it also has an obvious moral, and the good folk who were shocked by *Stalky*, forgave *Tom Brown* its brutalities for the sake of its moral, and never noticed that *Stalky* has its moral too, though of a subtler kind, and more decently hidden.

Incidentally, I have heard people doubt the wisdom of giving certain books of Kipling's, *Stalky* foremost among them, to children because of his Jingoistic tendencies. The old, old charge of Jingoism that has been levelled at him ever since Britain began to be ashamed of having (or having had) an Empire. The truth is that in all Kipling's works, even in such poems as *The White Man's Burden*, which sometimes sound odd and high-flown in our modern ears, the accent is not on dominion, but on service, and it does a child no harm to get the idea that service is not something to be ashamed of. And if anyone still doubts, let him, oh, do let him, read the chapter of *Stalky*, called *The Flag of their Country*, which concerns the doings of the Jelly-bellied Flag-flapper I have mentioned before, and in which Kipling paints a dazzling portrait of the kind of Jingoist he himself has been accused of being. The gentleman in question, an M.P. of vast unction and many chins, is addressing the school, very much against the school's will, on the subject of patriotism.

'In a raucous voice he cried aloud little matters like the hope of Honour and the dream of Glory, that boys do not discuss even with their most intimate equals; cheerfully assuming that, until he spoke, they had never considered these possibilities. He pointed them to shining goals, with fingers which smudged out all radiance on all horizons. He profaned the most secret places of their souls with outcries and gesticulations. He bade them consider the deeds of their ancestors in such fashion that they were flushed to their tingling ears. Some of them—the rending voice cut a frozen stillness—might have had relatives who perished in the defence of their country. (They thought, not a few of them, of an old sword in a passage, or above a breakfast-room table, seen and fingered by stealth since they could walk.) He adjured them to emulate those illustrious examples; and they looked all ways in their extreme discomfort.'

The reference to the sword and the breakfast-room shows how much of a period piece *Stalky* is now, but if the trappings have changed, the boys and the ideal exploits have not very much, and it remains one of the very few school stories which are also literature, and which I personally would try on any child in search of a boy's school story, whose reading I really cared about.

*　　*　　*　　*

The *Just So Stories* are as full of primitive noises as *Stalky*, and yet they, of all Kipling's stories, *must* be read aloud. Read to oneself they are poor things shorn of half their glory. Of what use is an incantation merely thought within one's head and not cried aloud to the stars? The *Just So Stories* are the true stuff of incantation and magic-making, with the inspired repetition of words and phrases ('You must *not* forget the suspenders, Best Beloved,') which is a necessary part of all the best magic and greatly beloved by most small children, though Dr Tompkins quotes one infant as saying in exasperation, 'You needn't say that again.' The first three-quarters of the book can be read to the very smallest children, and they will enjoy the incantation even if they do not always quite grasp what it is all about. This perhaps accounts for the fact that some of the stories have been issued separately in the U.S.A. in picture book form. The last two stories, *The Cat that Walked by Himself* and *The Butterfly that Stamped*, seem to me to be in a different category, possibly because they were written after small Josephine's death. They are more complex, and they go deeper than any of the earlier ones, except the two tales of Taffy and her father. *The Butterfly* is charming and exquisite, a story like a fragment of Eastern filigree work and luminous with a particularly lovely kind of laughter; the story of *The Cat*, seen in a kind of rainy witchlight, has a really back-hair-disturbing magic of its own. (But few children are disturbed by the things that seem to us to have the potency and terror of the true Other World; they keep their fears for the things that no adult would expect them to be afraid of. I know a pillar of the publishing world who admits to having been scared out of his wits by *Alice in Wonderland* when he was

seven. *I* had a spiritual horror of pearl buttons.
Neither of us felt anything about *The Cat that
Walked by Himself*, save that it was a very exciting
and very satisfying story and that the cat was
superbly catly.)

My own early favourites among the *Just So
Stories* were the two tales of Taffy and her father
Tegumai, the first largely because it made me
laugh until I curled up like an earwig, and the second
for the sake of that wonderful alphabet necklace,
chronicled bead by bead; but also because of the
sense of safety and being beloved which enfolds
the naughty small heroine, as though her father had
spread a cloak over his Little Girl-Daughter to
keep out the cold. I re-read the *Just So Stories*
before writing this, and was struck afresh by the
depth of feeling not so much in the story but flowing
out from it to the child for whom it was told, which
makes it almost painfully touching, when one
remembers small Josephine. Only twice in all his
writings, Kipling cries out for the lost child: once
in *They* and once in the song that goes with Taffy,
the song beginning, 'There runs a road by Merrow
Down', which ends,

'In mocassins and deerskin cloak,
Unfearing, free and fair she flits,

And lights her little damp-wood smoke
To show her Daddy where she flits

For far—oh, very far behind,
So far she cannot call to him,
Comes Tegumai alone to find
The daughter that was all to him.'

And to my mind, Taffy's song is the more moving
of the two.

Incidentally, like *Peter Rabbit*, the *Just So Stories*,
with their camels most 'scruciating idle, and their
Parsees with hats from which the rays of the sun
were reflected in more-than-Oriental-splendour,
are the answer to the people who think that one
should not use long words in writing for children.
Half the glory of the *Just So Stories*, as I remember
across thirty years, was the glory of their long words.
I didn't always (I didn't often) understand what
they meant, but that was not of the least conse-
quence. They tasted superb.

VIII. The Captains and the Kings

I did not come to *Captains Courageous* until well after I was grown up, and so my approach to it is quite different from my approach to any other of the books gathered here. I can stand back and look at it dispassionately, because I am not emotionally involved. I enjoyed it enormously for a wonderfully detailed account of life in the cod fisheries of the Grand Banks. I was deeply moved by the story of Penn, the 'half-caulked' member of the *We're Here*'s crew, who had been a Moravian pastor, and, seeing his wife and children killed by a flood before his eyes, had lost his identity. When, at another man's need, his memory returned for a space, I felt that I could not bear it; and when, the need being over, the memory and the man's dignity went again, leaving only poor little twittering half-caulked Penn behind, I could bear it less than ever. I suffered one of the coldest cold chills I have ever experienced when the two days dead and sea-buried French sailor returned to claim his brass-mounted knife with which he had killed a man, and I have read few more exciting 'speed pieces' than the account of the multi-millionaire's dash across America in his own private car (it took me some time to realise that it was what we should call a private railway coach) to meet his long-lost son. And yet *Captains Courageous* is the only one among the books dealt with here that I have never wanted to read again.

I was going to complain that there is no shape to the story, but neither is there any shape to speak of to *Kim*, and the moment I open *Kim*, for the third or the eighth or the dozenth time, something in me leaps up in the certainty that I am going to find delight in every page. *Captains Courageous* has no shimmering and crowding riches to compare with *Kim*, and no characters that spring out and lay hold and remain with one afterwards, as the other book has. Of the two boy heroes, Kim, through all his steady development of character, remains most gloriously and consistently and vividly Kim. But Harvey Cheyne, the unpleasant son of the multi-millionaire, having fallen overboard from his ship and been picked up by the *We're Here*, gives one exhibition of frightfulness, and being knocked into the scuppers by the Master, undergoes a change of heart so sudden as to be, to my mind, unconvincing, and becomes thereafter a different person.

Nevertheless, I should rate *Captains Courageous* as a fine story for any boy who likes to read about the sea and seafaring men. It will carry him along with the swing of the long sea swells from the first page to the last, and when he gets to the last page, any ideas that he has absorbed on the way will be sound ones.

Last of all, *Puck of Pook's Hill* and *Rewards and Fairies*, for like the *Jungle Books*, both *Puck* books must be considered together. In my childhood, I enjoyed *Puck of Pook's Hill* best. I have found that to be the case with most children, and the reason is simple; the stories were written for two real children, Kipling's own John and Elsie, who were the originals of Dan and Una, and they took more than five years to write. The children were only seven and eight when they made their play of Puck and Titania, with the paper donkey's head. They were thirteen and fourteen when *Rewards and Fairies* was published, and the stories had kept pace with them. And therefore, although both series follow on from each other and appear to be for the same age group, those in *Rewards* are actually way above the head of the child who is just able comfortably to manage those in *Puck of Pook's Hill*, not of course that one can really talk of age groups in this particular connection, since Kipling wrote his books on so many levels. As he himself writes of the *Puck* stories,

'I worked the material in three or four overlaid tints and textures, which might or might not reveal themselves according to the shifting light of sex, youth and experience. The tales had to be read by children, before people realised that they were meant for grown-ups.'

The fact remains that most of the children who delight in *Puck of Pook's Hill* will find *Rewards and Fairies* difficult, and have to come to it later.

It is a more highly evolved piece of work than *Puck*; there is in the first book nothing to touch the silver-point delicacy, the quietness as of a country seen in level evening light, of *Marklake Witches* with its haunting accompanying poem *The Way Through the Woods*, nothing that pierces as deep into the very root of things as the pathetic and terrible story of *The Knife and the Naked Chalk*, nothing to touch the rich irony of *The Wrong Thing*. Yet somehow one gets the impression that the first series was written 'as a bird sings' and the second series was not, and the things that one remembers most belong to the first book; Parnesius marching his cohort up to the old gateway into Valentia and finding the arch bricked up and *Finis* scrawled on the dead end; the vivid and most beautiful picture of Sir Richard Dalyngridge crossing the stream on his great white horse. The people of some of the later stories seem less memorable than those of the first book, more perfectly fashioned but less instantly alive. I have even been bored by the American stories. And the *Tree of Justice*, the last story of all, and the most difficult with its strange undertones, which I love and always have loved very greatly, more perhaps than any single story in *Puck of Pook's Hill*, is another tale told by Sir Richard. So perhaps after all, it is just that meeting Sir Richard and Parnesius first, all the later comers are thrown a little into their shadow.

But as Professor Carrington points out, neither Parnesius nor Sir Richard, Dan nor Una, nor even Puck, are the true heroes of the *Puck* books. The true hero is old Hobden, the hedger and past master in the delicate art of poaching, who typifies the tough, earthy life of the countryman, persisting, rooted in his own land, through all the rootless changes that come and go. For the true theme of both books is the Land and the People, the continuity of life; the twentieth-century shepherd linked with the poor puzzled Stone Age hero who bought protection for the sheep, and then found that he must pay not only with the agreed loss of an eye, but with the cold burden of Godhead. Mr

Springett the builder's tale of saving the Squire from an unwanted ha ha, which so exactly echoes the story of Sir Harry Dawe's knighthood, across four hundred years. The watermill below the forge that both Parnesius and Sir Richard knew. . . .

And that is one of the greatest values of both books. Children are prone to grow up seeing history as a series of small static pictures, all belonging to Then and having nothing to do with Now. The two *Puck* books, stories and songs alike, with their linking of past and present in one corner of England, must help them to feel it as a living and continuous process of which they themselves are a part, must help them to be at least a little aware of their own living roots behind them, and so see their own times in better perspective than they might otherwise have done.

ix. Kipling Today

It has been a labour of delight to me to put together this short sketch of Kipling as a writer for children, because of all the writers of my childhood, he made the strongest impact on me, an impact which I have never forgotten. There were other books that I loved as much: *The Wind in the Willows*, *Winnie the Pooh*, *Hero Myths and Legends of the British Race*, and a slim, tattered copy of Hans Andersen's *Little Mermaid*, spring to my mind at once; also Lord Lytton's *Last Days of Pompeii*, which now strikes me as the most depressing piece of long-winded Victoriana. But never more than one book or story by any particular author, and never any that have stayed with me more vividly.

Mowgli and Bagheera (but chiefly Bagheera) enriched my make-believe world. *Stalky* and the *Just So Stories* furnished me with things to chant. Parnesius gave me my first feeling for Roman Britain, filling my small opening mind with a splendour as of distant trumpets, long before I had the least idea what the Roman Empire was all about, and when I pictured Maximus's white buckskin leggings laced with gold as being exactly like the knee-high gaiters with buttons all up the sides, in which my own unwilling legs were encased in the winter.

But all that was twenty-five or thirty years ago, and some of the stories were dated even then, though the dating is all on the surface and never in the fundamental things. The question then arises: what is Kipling's place in the world of children's literature today?

Miss Eileen Colwell, who is the Children's Librarian of the Borough of Hendon, suggests that in this country he lives mainly by virtue of the *Just So Stories* and the *Jungle Books*, both of which are used in library story-hours, often read by teachers to their classes, included in school reading lists, and bestowed on children by parents who loved them in their own childhood. And with the children themselves, from the ages of six to twelve, all three books are very popular. The favourite *Just So* story is undoubtedly *How the Elephant got his Trunk*. As one eight-year-old boy explained, 'The elephant story was the best, because he spanked all his relations.' Of the stories included in the *Jungle Books*, a ten-year-old girl chooses, just as I did myself at her age, *Rikki-Tikki-Tavy* and *The White Seal*; but *Toomai of the Elephants* seems to be the general favourite, though a good proportion of the boys, many of them Wolf Cubs themselves, prefer the Mowgli Stories. *Kim* is only for the out-of-the-ordinary child, and the same applies to *Captains Courageous*; while one eleven-year-old, asked by one of Miss Colwell's branch librarians for his opinion of *Stalky & Co.*, said that his Dad had told him it was a school story, but it wasn't a bit like any other school story he had read.

Puck of Pook's Hill and *Rewards and Fairies* are, sad to say, in almost total eclipse. The schools make no use of them, which seems surprising, and the children say that they dislike short stories, at any rate on historical subjects; and complain that fairies (Puck) are childish. This last reveals a particularly sorry state of affairs, since Puck, despite the canterbury-bell hat, which I have always myself felt to be regrettable, belongs to the true, fairy kind, the ancient aristocracy of the Lordly Ones, the People of the Hills; and such a criticism, levelled at him blindly, shows the damage that has been done by certain children's writers, who by their artless tales of tinsel-and-flower-petal creatures and wee, wee pixies living in wee, wee toadstool houses, have brought his whole race into disrepute, and robbed the modern child of a host of splendours.

There it is; a somewhat disappointing, though challenging picture to a Kipling addict such as myself. But strangely enough, in parts of the world in which one would expect children to be more essentially modern in outlook, and impatient of tradition, more aware of the dating in fact, the picture is a good deal brighter. The Librarian in charge of the Public Library Service to Children in Toronto (where in the children's rooms and school libraries, there are children of every nationality, race and colour), tells me that Kipling is a very favourite subject for library talks, that the *Jungle Books* and *Just So Stories* are constantly used in story-hours, while the books themselves are scarcely ever on the shelves. She also reports some of the children's views, notably one boy on *Captains Courageous*: 'It's a great story! The kid's stuck on himself and he smokes a cigarette and falls overboard and he thinks he can buy off the men on the other boat to take him home. Is he ever spoilt! It's great, you should read it!' A younger one on the *Jungle Books*: 'I like Kipling's books better than any others. I like the way they call it the Red Flower when they mean fire.' And a twelve-year-old with a sister of ten to whom one's heart goes out in sympathy: 'She doesn't like *Stalky*, so I'm reading it to her. I *want* her to like it. I love it.'

Kipling has so much to give to children still, of the things that do not date at all; worthwhile values to set against those of the horror comic; a rich and evocative use of language; stories, never ordinary, in which, because of that gift of his for writing about all things and people from the inside out instead of from the outside in, it is especially easy for the reader or read-to to perform the minor miracle of self-identification which so much helps a small growing mind to stretch itself and open out.

By no means every child will like Kipling, even his *Jungle Books* and *Just So Stories*; and those for whom the penny does not drop and the bell does not ring, will probably dislike him very much indeed, for he is one of those writers about whom there can be no half measures. But every child should have a chance, by having one or other of the books put into his hands at the right moment, to discover for himself whether he likes Kipling or not. Because the child who has never run with Mowgli's wolfpack, or stood with Parnesius and Pertinax to defend the Northern Wall, or thrust a very dead cat under the floor of a rival dormitory to the full length of his arm and Beetle's brolly, has missed something that he will not get from any other writer.

Books by Rudyard Kipling which are now available of interest to children

ALL KIPLING'S PROSE WORKS ARE PUBLISHED IN THE UNITED KINGDOM BY MESSRS MACMILLAN & CO LTD

Title	Date of first publication	Present available editions
The Jungle Book	1894	Library Edition. Illustrated. Ex. crown 8vo.
		Young People's Edition. Illustrated. Ex. crown 8vo.
		Pocket Edition. Illustrated. F'cap 8vo.
		School Edition. Gl. 8vo.
The Second Jungle Book	1895	Library Edition. Illustrated. Ex. crown 8vo.
		Young People's Edition. Illustrated. Ex. crown 8vo.
		Pocket Edition. Illustrated. F'cap 8vo.
		Overseas Edition. Crown 8vo.
		School Edition. Gl. 8vo.
Captains Courageous	1896–7	Library Edition. Illustrated. Ex. crown 8vo.
		Young People's Edition. Illustrated. Ex. crown 8vo.
		Pocket Edition. Illustrated. F'cap 8vo.
		School Edition. Gl. 8vo.
Stalky & Co.	1899	Library Edition. Illustrated. Ex. crown 8vo.
		Young People's Edition. Illustrated. Ex. crown 8vo.
		Pocket Edition. Illustrated. F'cap 8vo.
Kim	1900–1	Illustrated by Stuart Tresilian. Demy 8vo.
		Library Edition. Illustrated. Ex. crown 8vo.
		Young People's Edition. Illustrated. Ex. crown 8vo.
		Pocket Edition. Illustrated. F'cap 8vo.
		School Edition. Gl. 8vo.

Just So Stories	1902	Illustrated by the author. 4to.
		Library Edition. Illustrated. Ex. crown 8vo.
		Young People's Edition. Illustrated. F'cap 8vo.
		Pocket Edition. Illustrated. F'cap 8vo.
		School Edition. Gl. 8vo.
Puck of Pook's Hill	1906	Library Edition. Illustrated. Ex. crown 8vo.
		Young People's Edition. Illustrated. Ex. crown 8vo.
		Pocket Edition. Illustrated. F'cap 8vo.
		Overseas Edition. Crown 8vo.
		School Edition. Gl. 8vo.
Rewards and Fairies	1910	Library Edition. Illustrated. Ex. crown 8vo.
		Young People's Edition. Illustrated. Ex. crown 8vo.
		Pocket Edition. Illustrated. F'cap 8vo.
Animal Stories (compiled as follows:)	1932	Illustrated by Stuart Tresilian. Crown 4to.

The Camel's Hump (poem) from *Just So Stories*
The Cat that Walked by Himself from *Just So Stories*
Pussy Can Sit by the Fire and Sing (poem) from *Just So Stories*
The Conversion of St. Wilfrid from *Rewards and Fairies*
Garm, a Hostage from *Actions and Reactions*
The White Seal from *The Jungle Book*
The Maltese Cat from *The Day's Work*
Lukannon (poem) from *The Jungle Book*
How Fear Came from *The Second Jungle Book*
The Law of the Jungle (poem) from *The Second Jungle Book*
My Lord the Elephant from *Many Inventions*
I Keep Six Honest Serving Men (poem) from *Just So Stories*
Rikki-Tikki-Tavy from *The Jungle Book*
Darzee's Chaunt (poem) from *The Jungle Book*
Moti Guj—Mutineer from *Life's Handicap*
I Will Remember What I Was (poem) from *The Jungle Book*
Private Learoyd's Story from *Soldiers Three*
Toomai of the Elephants from *The Jungle Book*
Parade Song of the Camp Animals (poem) from *The Jungle Book*

| *All the Mowgli Stories* 1933 (compiled from *The Jungle Book* and *The Second Jungle Book*) | Illustrated by Stuart Tresilian. Crown 4to. |
| *The Maltese Cat* 1955 | Illustrated by Lionel Edwards. Pott. 4to. |

Books by Rudyard Kipling of interest to children which are now available in the United States.

The Jungle Book. (Century, 1899. Now published by Doubleday)

The Second Jungle Book. (Century, 1895. Now published by Doubleday)

Captains Courageous. (Century, 1897. Now published by Doubleday)

Stalky & Co. (Doubleday, 1899)

Kim. (Doubleday, 1901)

Just So Stories. (Doubleday, 1902)

Puck of Pook's Hill. (Doubleday, 1906)

Rewards and Fairies. (Doubleday, 1910)

All the Mowgli Stories. (Compiled from *The Jungle Book* and *The Second Jungle Book.* Doubleday, 1936)

The Maltese Cat. (Doubleday, 1936)